To

_____

From

_____

LIVING
AT THE NEXT
LEVEL

Insights for
Reaching Your Dreams

JOHN C. MAXWELL

THOMAS NELSON PUBLISHERS
Nashville • Atlanta • London • Vancouver

Published in Nashville, Tennessee, by Thomas Nelson, Inc., and distributed
in Canada by Word Communications, Ltd., Richmond, British Columbia,
and in the United Kingdom by Word (UK), Ltd., Milton Keynes, England.

Scripture quotations are from the CONTEMPORARY ENGLISH
VERSION of the Bible © 1991, 1995 by the American Bible Society. Used
by permission.

Library of Congress Cataloging-in-Publication Data

Maxwell, John C., 1947–
    Living at the next level : insights for reaching your dreams / John C.
Maxwell.
        p.   cm.
    ISBN 0-7852-7267-4 (hc)
    1. S:uccess—Quotations, maxims, etc.
BJ1611.M473   1996
158'.1—dc20   96-9167
                                                              CIP

Printed in the United States of America
1 2 3 4 5 6 7 - 02 01 00 99 98 97 96

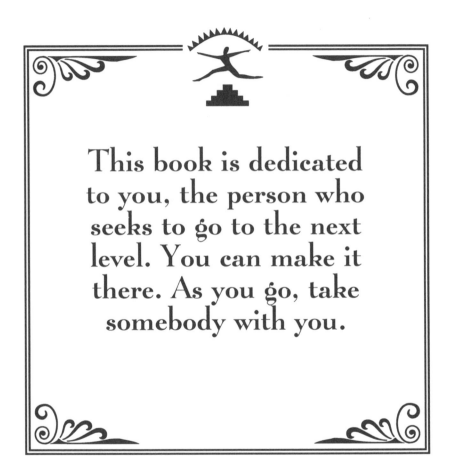

This book is dedicated to you, the person who seeks to go to the next level. You can make it there. As you go, take somebody with you.

Introduction

What does it mean to live at the next level?

Many people think there's a great gap separating those who live an ordinary life and those who live an extraordinary one. But the truth is that there's only a fine line between where you are now and the next level. Sometimes all it takes to move up is a small change in your daily habits, a little different way of looking at things, or a willingness to get up one more time than you've been knocked down. The only real difference between ordinary and extraordinary is that little "extra."

In the following pages you'll find a collection of quotes to motivate and encourage you to move up to the next level. No matter where you are right now, you're capable of taking that step. The key is to do what you can *today* to come closer to your potential *tomorrow*. Do that and before you know it, you'll find that you've moved up to the next level—and that you're becoming the person you were meant to be.

Keep growing. And I'll see you at the next level!

John Maxwell
San Diego

LIVING
AT THE NEXT
LEVEL

Insights for Reaching Your Dreams

The road to the next level is always uphill.

— JOHN MAXWELL

How have you changed . . . lately? In the last week, let's say? Or the last month? The last year? Can you be very specific?

— HOWARD HENDRICKS

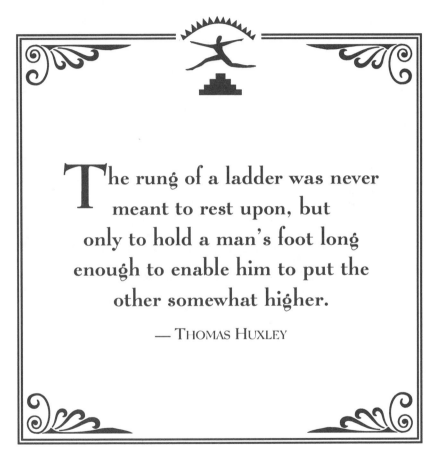

The rung of a ladder was never meant to rest upon, but only to hold a man's foot long enough to enable him to put the other somewhat higher.

— THOMAS HUXLEY

I f you keep doing what you've always done, you'll always get what you've always gotten.

— JOHN MAXWELL

4

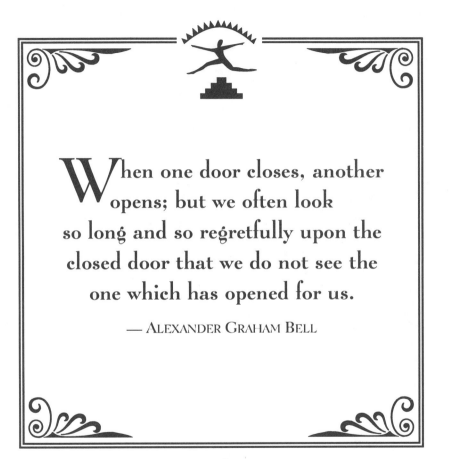

When one door closes, another
opens; but we often look
so long and so regretfully upon the
closed door that we do not see the
one which has opened for us.

— ALEXANDER GRAHAM BELL

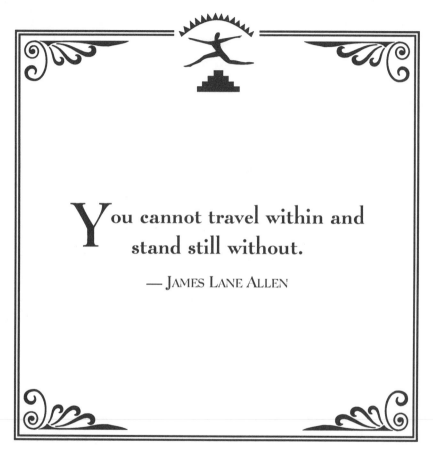

You cannot travel within and stand still without.

— JAMES LANE ALLEN

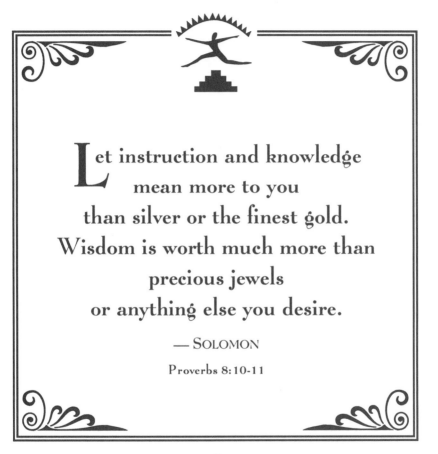

Let instruction and knowledge
mean more to you
than silver or the finest gold.
Wisdom is worth much more than
precious jewels
or anything else you desire.

— SOLOMON

Proverbs 8:10-11

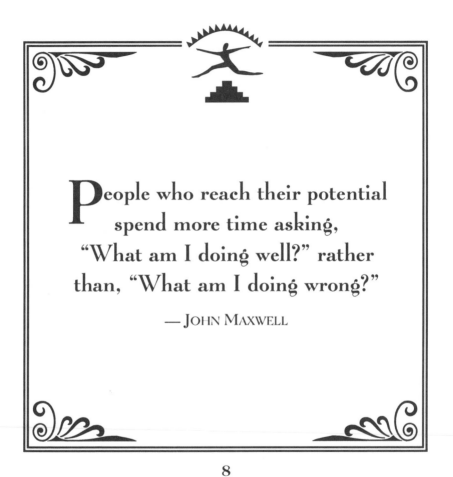

People who reach their potential
spend more time asking,
"What am I doing well?" rather
than, "What am I doing wrong?"

— John Maxwell

Never let the fear of striking out get in your way.

— BABE RUTH

I t's not what you are going to do,
but it's what you are doing
now that counts.

— NAPOLEON HILL

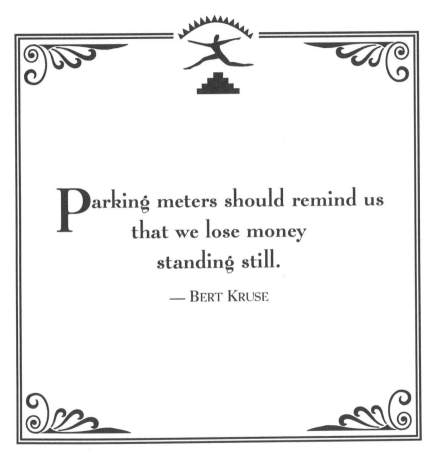

Parking meters should remind us
that we lose money
standing still.

— BERT KRUSE

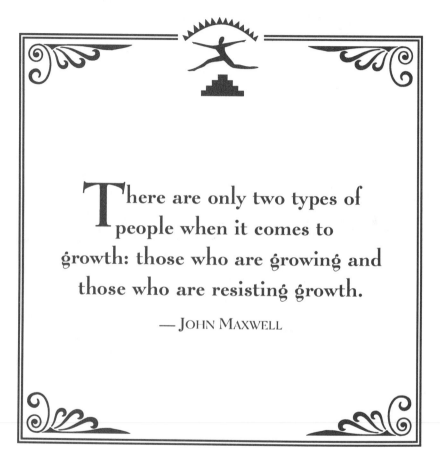

There are only two types of people when it comes to growth: those who are growing and those who are resisting growth.

— JOHN MAXWELL

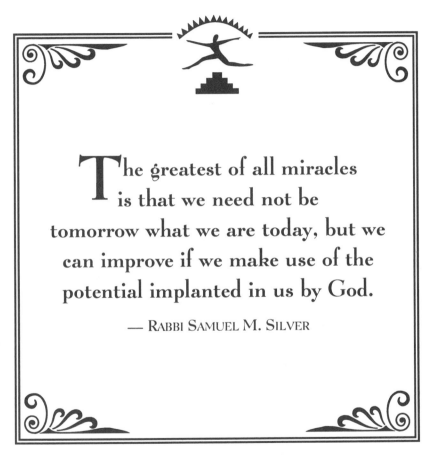

The greatest of all miracles
is that we need not be
tomorrow what we are today, but we
can improve if we make use of the
potential implanted in us by God.

— RABBI SAMUEL M. SILVER

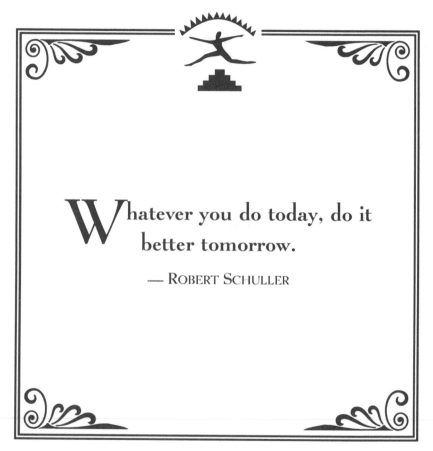

W hatever you do today, do it better tomorrow.

— ROBERT SCHULLER

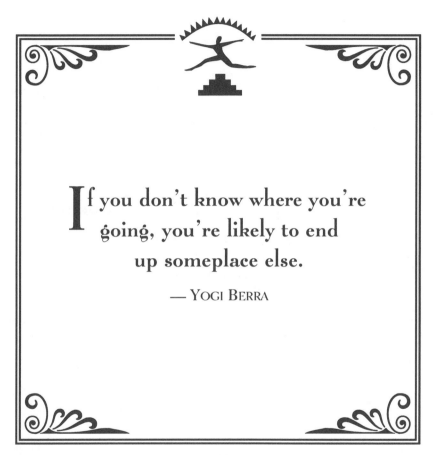

I f you don't know where you're
going, you're likely to end
up someplace else.

— YOGI BERRA

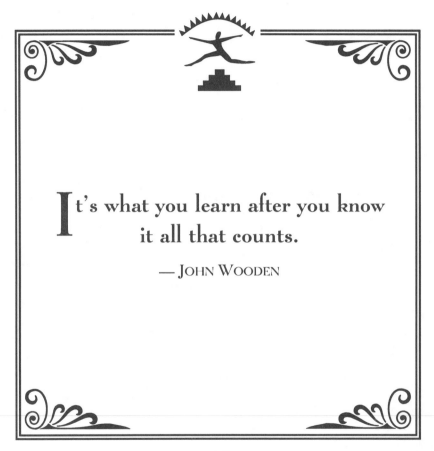

I t's what you learn after you know
it all that counts.

— JOHN WOODEN

S mall opportunities are often the beginning of great enterprises.

— DEMOSTHENES

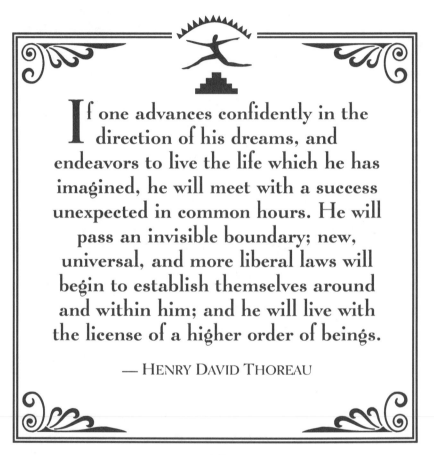

If one advances confidently in the direction of his dreams, and endeavors to live the life which he has imagined, he will meet with a success unexpected in common hours. He will pass an invisible boundary; new, universal, and more liberal laws will begin to establish themselves around and within him; and he will live with the license of a higher order of beings.

— HENRY DAVID THOREAU

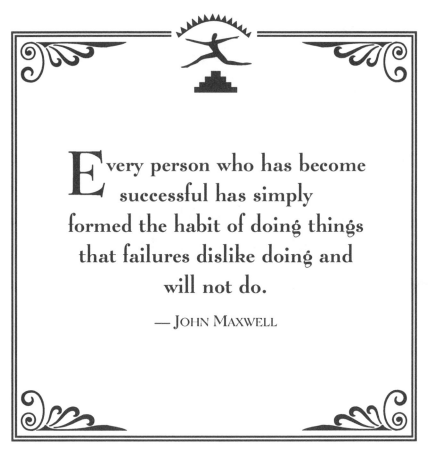

E very person who has become
successful has simply
formed the habit of doing things
that failures dislike doing and
will not do.

— JOHN MAXWELL

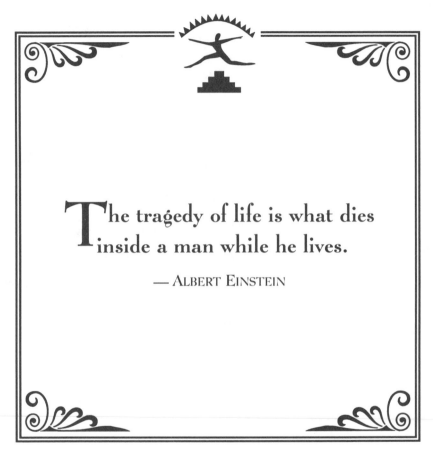

The tragedy of life is what dies
inside a man while he lives.

— ALBERT EINSTEIN

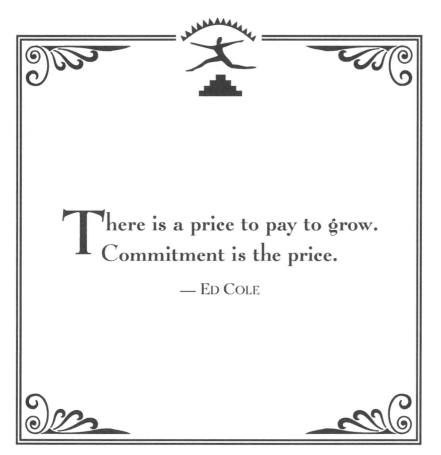

There is a price to pay to grow.
Commitment is the price.

— ED COLE

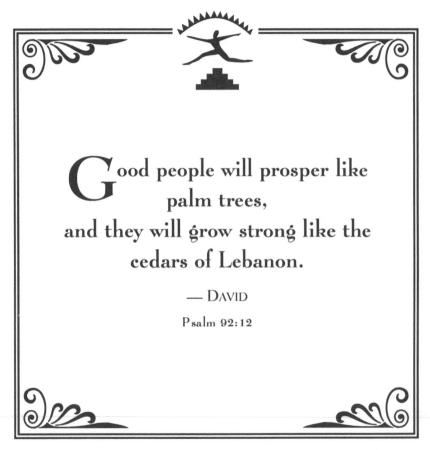

Good people will prosper like
palm trees,
and they will grow strong like the
cedars of Lebanon.

— DAVID

Psalm 92:12

22

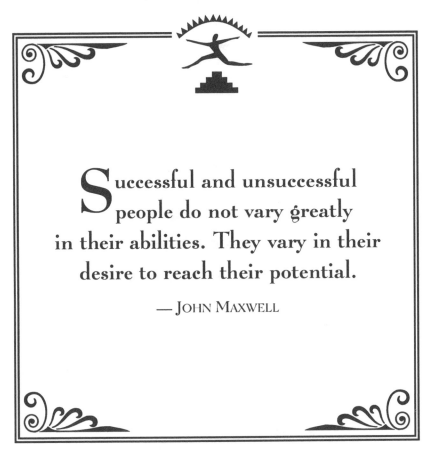

S uccessful and unsuccessful
people do not vary greatly
in their abilities. They vary in their
desire to reach their potential.

— JOHN MAXWELL

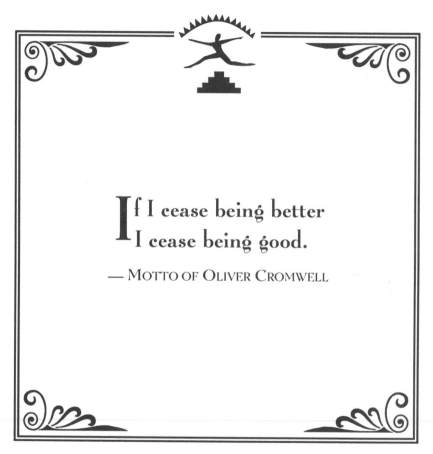

I f I cease being better
I cease being good.

— MOTTO OF OLIVER CROMWELL

U nless you try to do something
beyond what you have
already mastered, you will
never grow.

— RONALD E. OSBORN

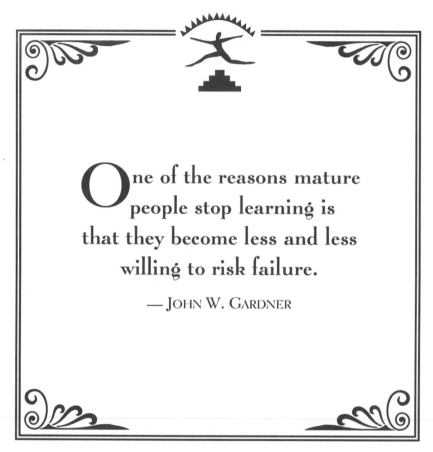

One of the reasons mature people stop learning is that they become less and less willing to risk failure.

— JOHN W. GARDNER

For everything you gain,
you lose something.

— RALPH WALDO EMERSON

If you aren't making any mistakes,
it's a sure sign you're playing
it too safe.

— JOHN MAXWELL

L ife is either a daring adventure
or nothing.

— HELEN KELLER

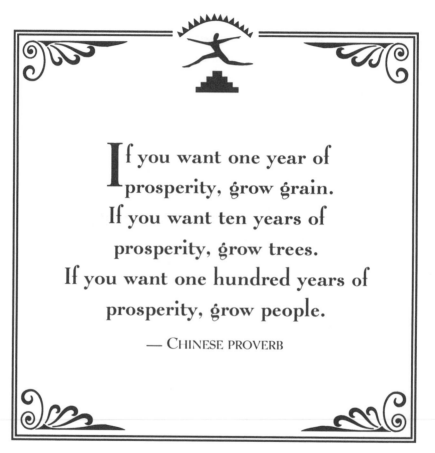

If you want one year of prosperity, grow grain.
If you want ten years of prosperity, grow trees.
If you want one hundred years of prosperity, grow people.

— CHINESE PROVERB

A wise man will make more
opportunities than
he finds.

— SIR FRANCIS BACON

31

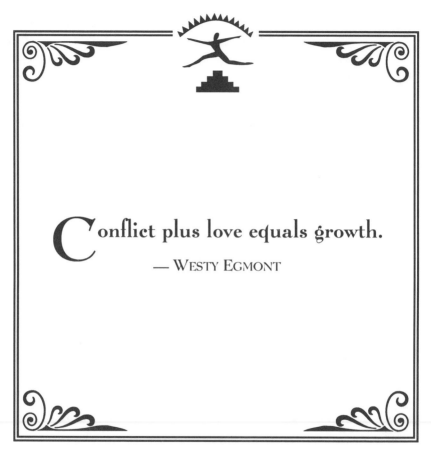

Conflict plus love equals growth.

— WESTY EGMONT

I f your vision doesn't cost you something, it's a daydream.

— JOHN MAXWELL

As long as you're green, you're growing; as soon as you're ripe, you start to rot.

— RAY KROC

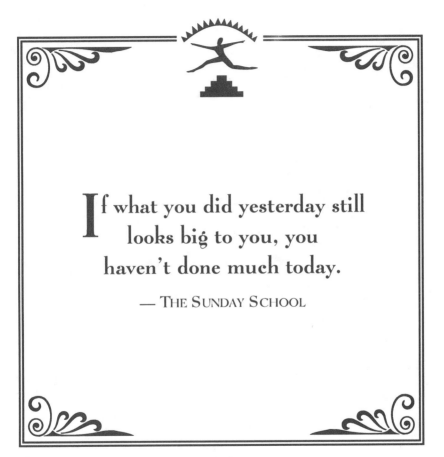

I f what you did yesterday still looks big to you, you haven't done much today.

— THE SUNDAY SCHOOL

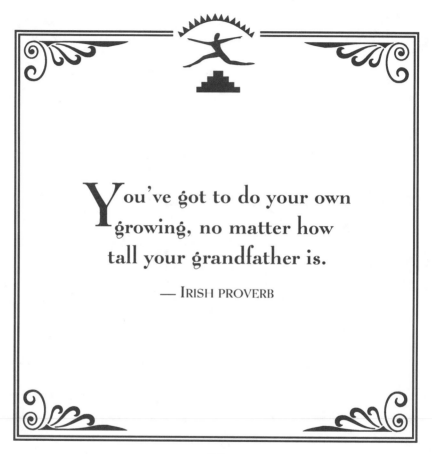

Y ou've got to do your own
growing, no matter how
tall your grandfather is.

— IRISH PROVERB

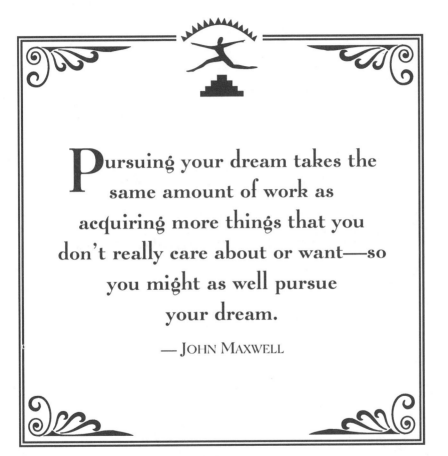

Pursuing your dream takes the
same amount of work as
acquiring more things that you
don't really care about or want—so
you might as well pursue
your dream.

— JOHN MAXWELL

The greatest achievements are those that benefit others.

— Denis Waitley

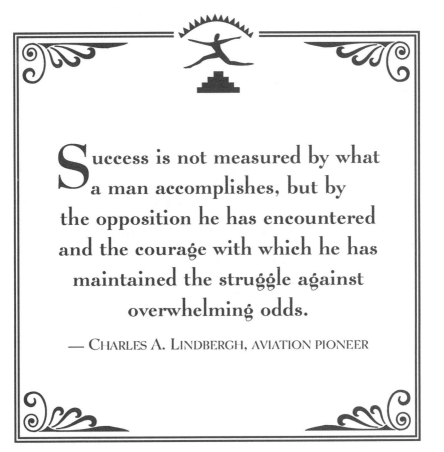

Success is not measured by what a man accomplishes, but by the opposition he has encountered and the courage with which he has maintained the struggle against overwhelming odds.

— CHARLES A. LINDBERGH, AVIATION PIONEER

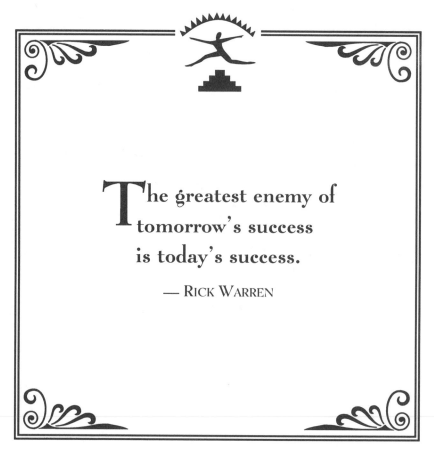

The greatest enemy of
tomorrow's success
is today's success.

— RICK WARREN

To improve is to change; to be perfect is to change often.

— WINSTON CHURCHILL

41

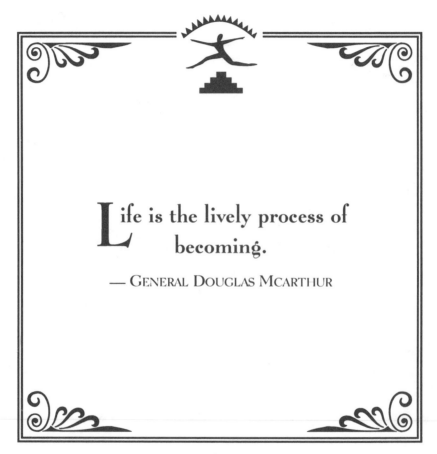

L ife is the lively process of becoming.

— GENERAL DOUGLAS MCARTHUR

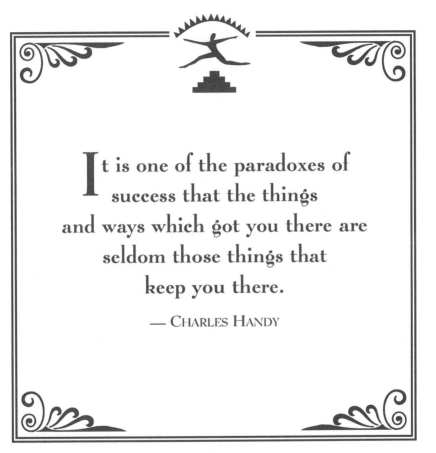

It is one of the paradoxes of
success that the things
and ways which got you there are
seldom those things that
keep you there.

— CHARLES HANDY

43

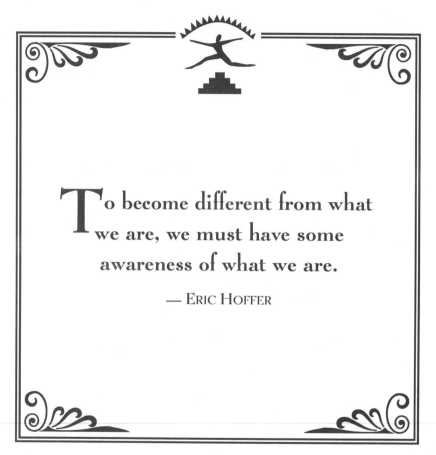

To become different from what
we are, we must have some
awareness of what we are.

— ERIC HOFFER

Too many people stop growing when the price gets too high.

— JOHN MAXWELL

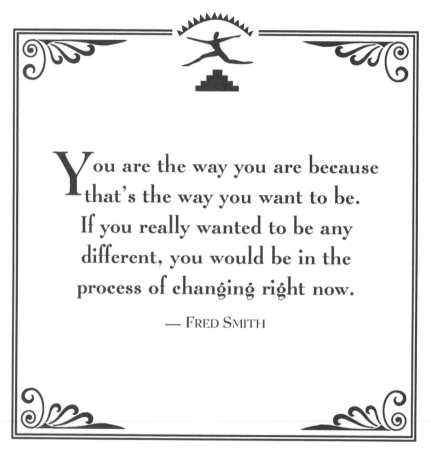

You are the way you are because that's the way you want to be. If you really wanted to be any different, you would be in the process of changing right now.

— FRED SMITH

You've got to continue to grow, or you're just like last night's cornbread—stale and dry.

— LORETTA LYNN

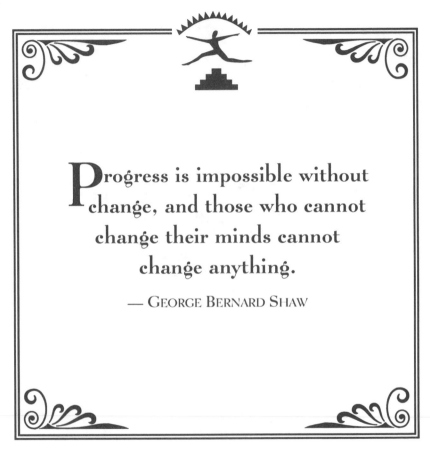

Progress is impossible without change, and those who cannot change their minds cannot change anything.

— GEORGE BERNARD SHAW

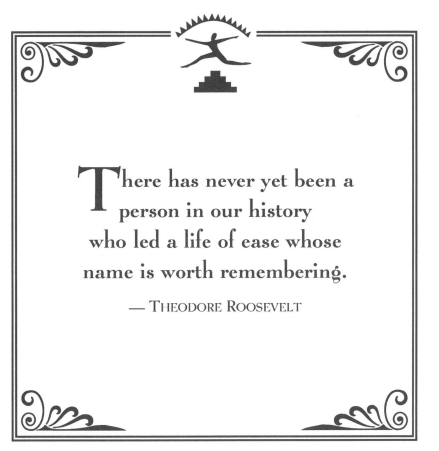

There has never yet been a
person in our history
who led a life of ease whose
name is worth remembering.

— THEODORE ROOSEVELT

Shortcuts never pay off in the long run.

— JOHN MAXWELL

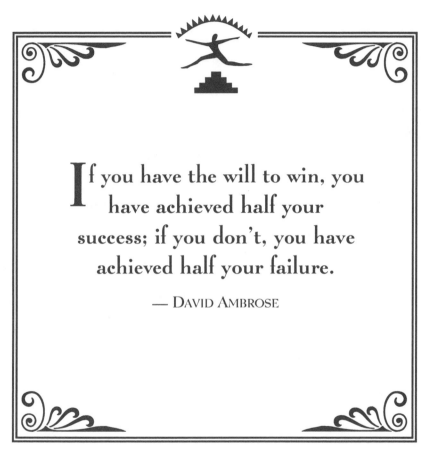

If you have the will to win, you
have achieved half your
success; if you don't, you have
achieved half your failure.

— DAVID AMBROSE

Change itself is not progress, but change is the price that we pay for progress.

— CLAYTON G. ORCUTT

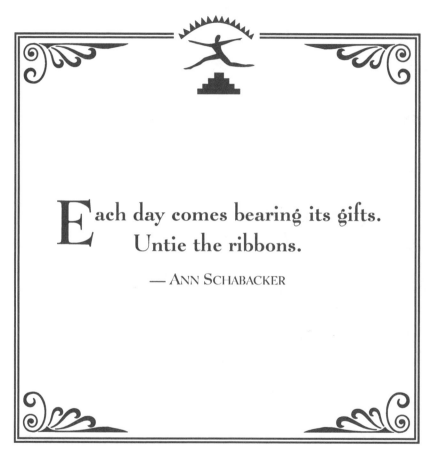

Each day comes bearing its gifts.
Untie the ribbons.

— ANN SCHABACKER

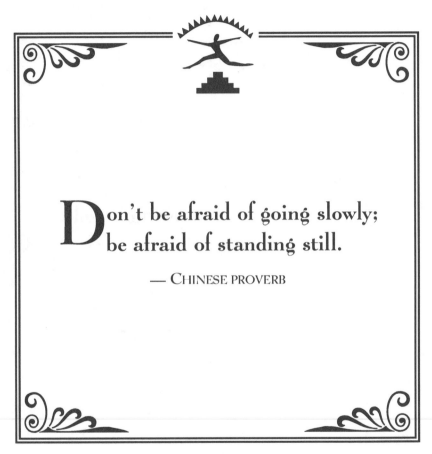

D on't be afraid of going slowly;
be afraid of standing still.

— CHINESE PROVERB

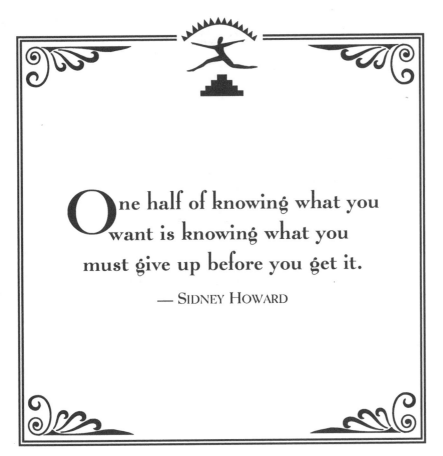

One half of knowing what you want is knowing what you must give up before you get it.

— Sidney Howard

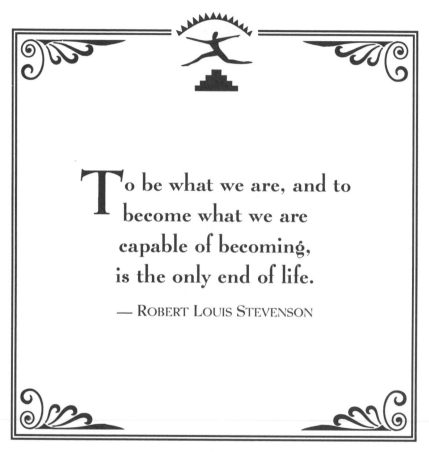

To be what we are, and to
become what we are
capable of becoming,
is the only end of life.

— ROBERT LOUIS STEVENSON

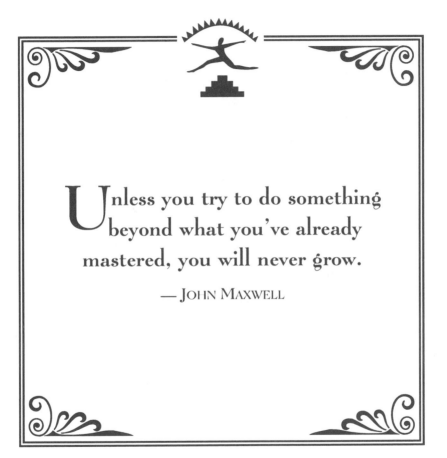

Unless you try to do something beyond what you've already mastered, you will never grow.

— JOHN MAXWELL

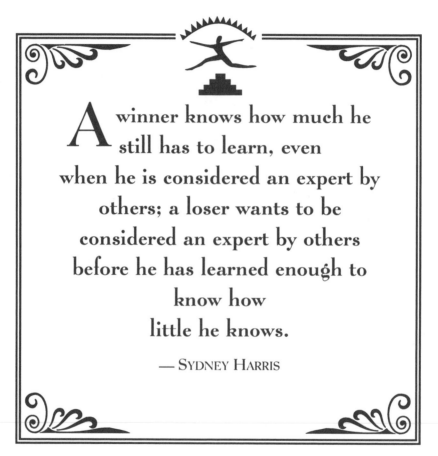

A winner knows how much he still has to learn, even when he is considered an expert by others; a loser wants to be considered an expert by others before he has learned enough to know how little he knows.

— SYDNEY HARRIS

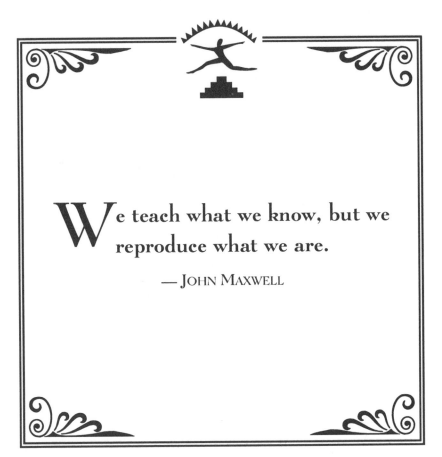

We teach what we know, but we reproduce what we are.

— JOHN MAXWELL

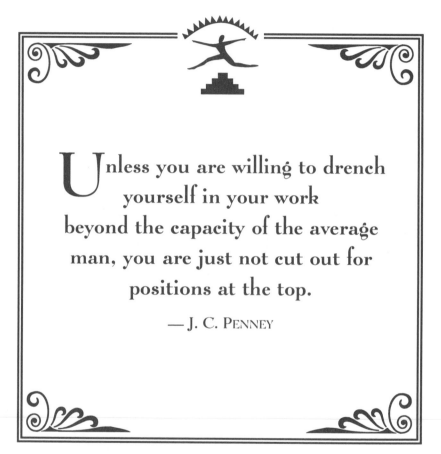

U nless you are willing to drench
yourself in your work
beyond the capacity of the average
man, you are just not cut out for
positions at the top.

— J. C. PENNEY

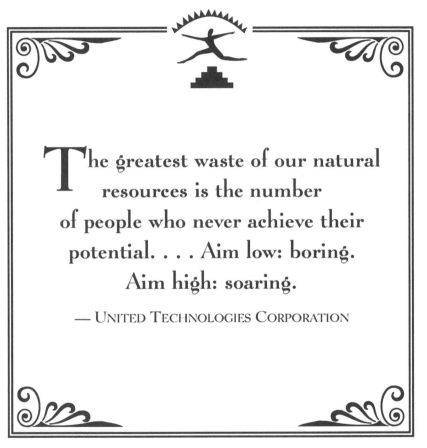

The greatest waste of our natural
resources is the number
of people who never achieve their
potential. . . . Aim low: boring.
Aim high: soaring.

— UNITED TECHNOLOGIES CORPORATION

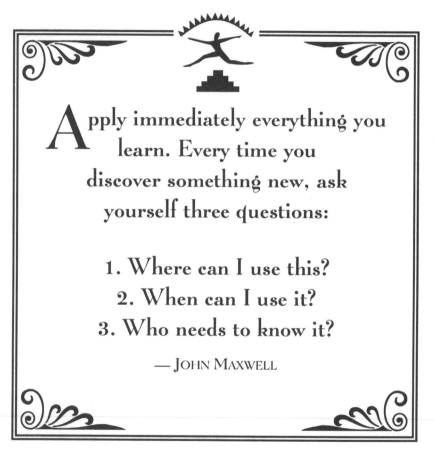

Apply immediately everything you learn. Every time you discover something new, ask yourself three questions:

1. Where can I use this?
2. When can I use it?
3. Who needs to know it?

— JOHN MAXWELL

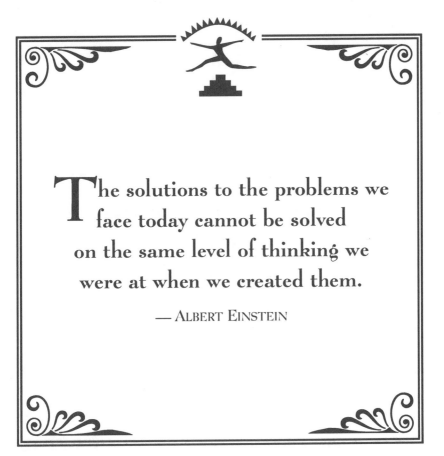

The solutions to the problems we
face today cannot be solved
on the same level of thinking we
were at when we created them.

— ALBERT EINSTEIN

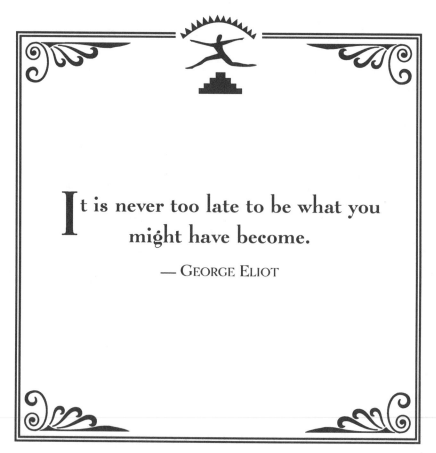

It is never too late to be what you might have become.

— GEORGE ELIOT

We grow
by
dreams.

— WOODROW WILSON

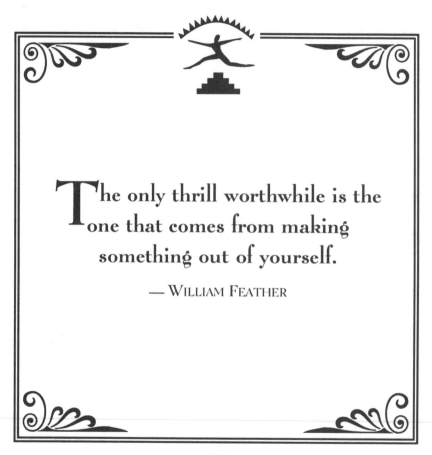

The only thrill worthwhile is the one that comes from making something out of yourself.

— WILLIAM FEATHER

Respect and obey the LORD!
This is the beginning
of wisdom.
To have understanding, you must
know the Holy God.

— SOLOMON

Proverbs 9:10

A

ll achievements require time.

— David Joseph Schwartz

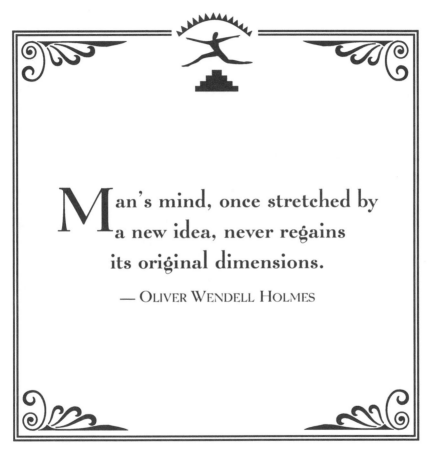

M an's mind, once stretched by
a new idea, never regains
its original dimensions.

— OLIVER WENDELL HOLMES

When you do the things you ought to do when you ought to do them, the day will come when you will do the things you want to do when you want to do them.

— ZIG ZIGLAR

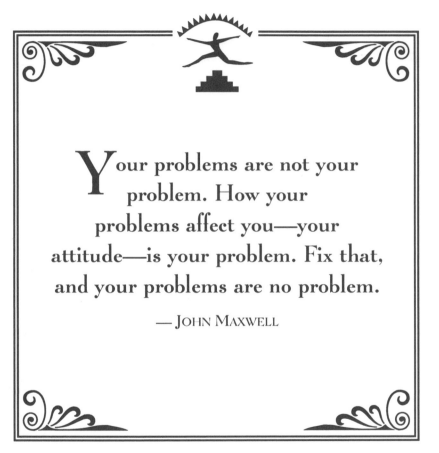

Your problems are not your problem. How your problems affect you—your attitude—is your problem. Fix that, and your problems are no problem.

— JOHN MAXWELL

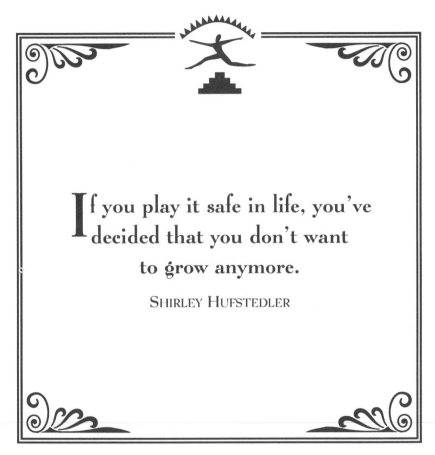

I f you play it safe in life, you've
decided that you don't want
to grow anymore.

SHIRLEY HUFSTEDLER

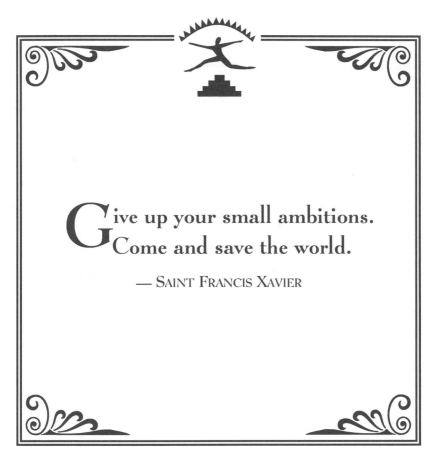

Give up your small ambitions.
Come and save the world.

— Saint Francis Xavier

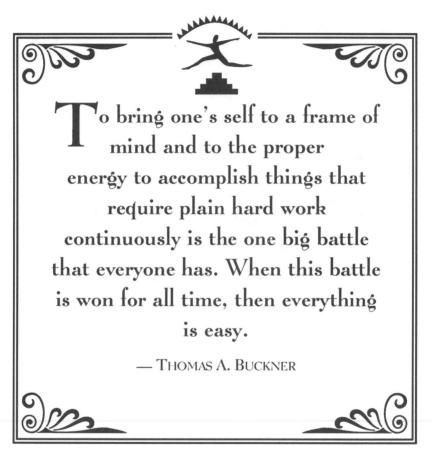

To bring one's self to a frame of
mind and to the proper
energy to accomplish things that
require plain hard work
continuously is the one big battle
that everyone has. When this battle
is won for all time, then everything
is easy.

— THOMAS A. BUCKNER

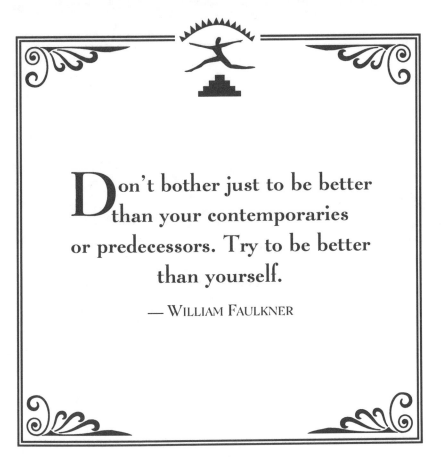

Don't bother just to be better than your contemporaries or predecessors. Try to be better than yourself.

— WILLIAM FAULKNER

The starting point of all achievement is desire.

— NAPOLEON HILL

Failure is not fatal. Only failure
to get back up is.

— JOHN MAXWELL

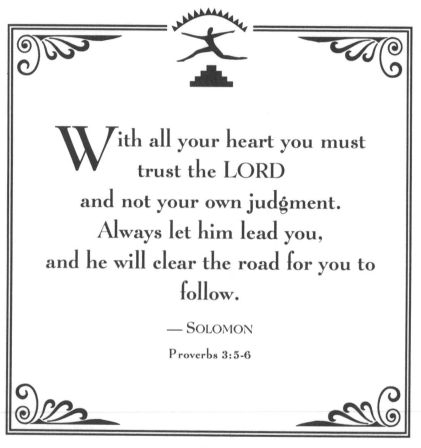

With all your heart you must trust the LORD
and not your own judgment.
Always let him lead you,
and he will clear the road for you to
follow.

— SOLOMON

Proverbs 3:5-6

Only those who dare to fail
greatly can ever
achieve greatly.

— ROBERT KENNEDY

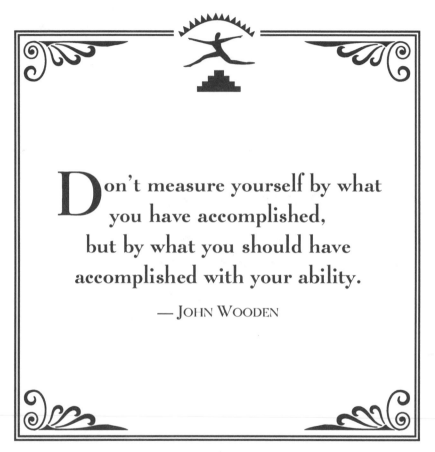

Don't measure yourself by what you have accomplished,
but by what you should have accomplished with your ability.

— JOHN WOODEN

Things may come to those who
wait, but only the things left
by those who hustle.

— ABRAHAM LINCOLN

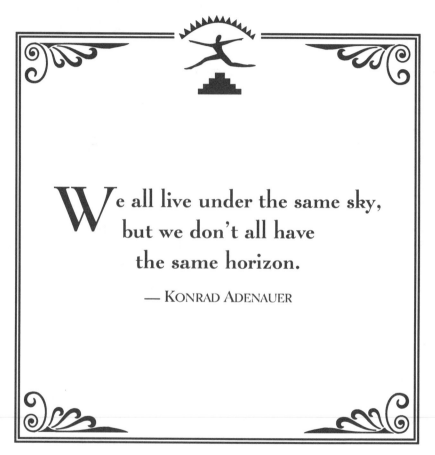

W e all live under the same sky,
but we don't all have
the same horizon.

— KONRAD ADENAUER

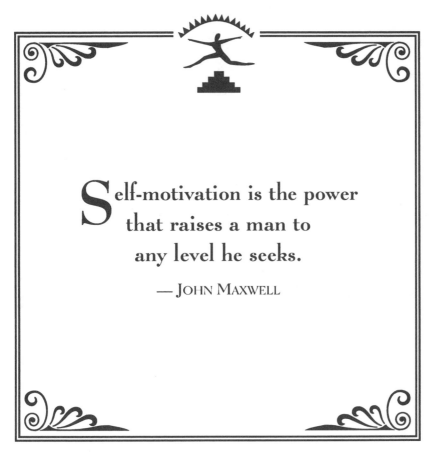

Self-motivation is the power
that raises a man to
any level he seeks.

— JOHN MAXWELL

One doesn't discover new lands
without consenting to
lose sight of the shore for a
very long time.

— ANDRÉ GIDE

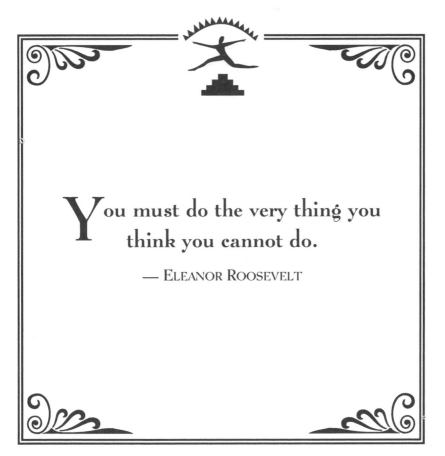

Y ou must do the very thing you
think you cannot do.

— ELEANOR ROOSEVELT

When you're through changing, you're through.

— BRUCE BARTON

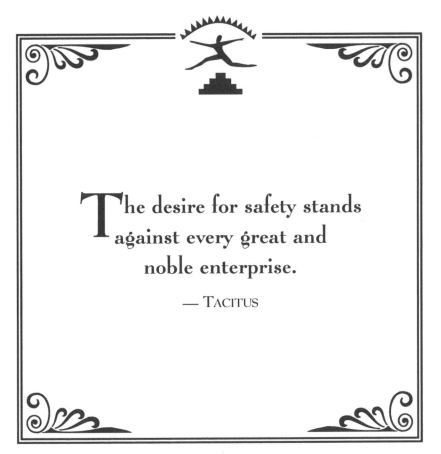

The desire for safety stands against every great and noble enterprise.

— TACITUS

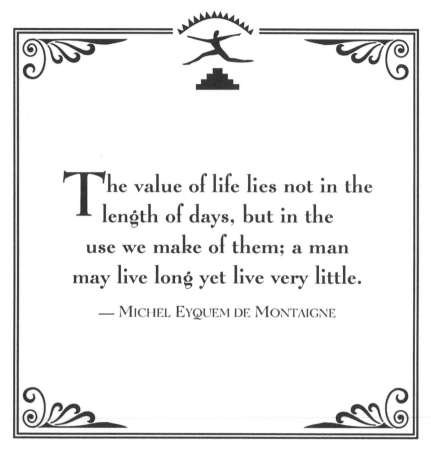

The value of life lies not in the length of days, but in the use we make of them; a man may live long yet live very little.

— MICHEL EYQUEM DE MONTAIGNE

Only he who keeps his eye fixed
on the far horizon will find
his right road.

— DAG HAMMARSKJOLD

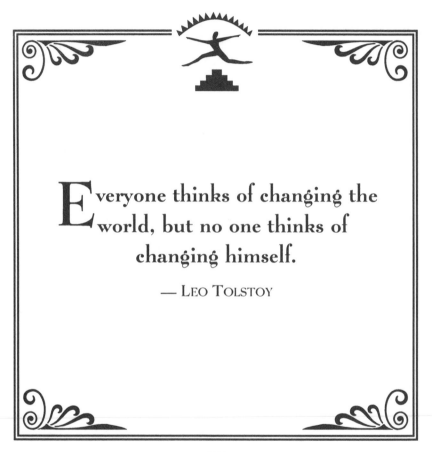

Everyone thinks of changing the world, but no one thinks of changing himself.

— LEO TOLSTOY

Every opportunity to fear is also an opportunity to trust God.

— JOHN MAXWELL

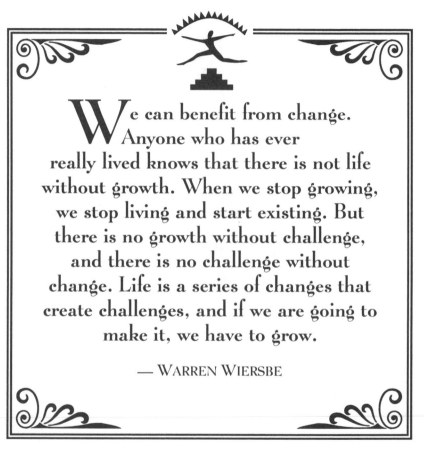

We can benefit from change. Anyone who has ever really lived knows that there is not life without growth. When we stop growing, we stop living and start existing. But there is no growth without challenge, and there is no challenge without change. Life is a series of changes that create challenges, and if we are going to make it, we have to grow.

— WARREN WIERSBE

The great use of life is to spend it for something that will outlast it.

— CHARLES MAYES

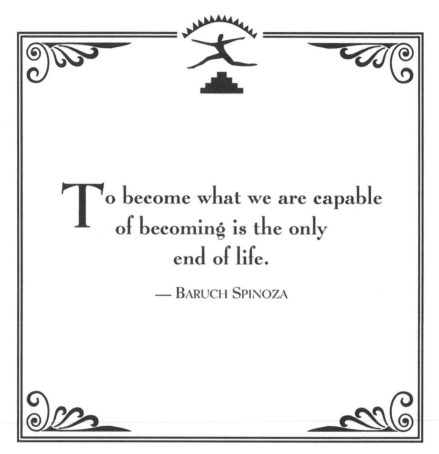

To become what we are capable
of becoming is the only
end of life.

— BARUCH SPINOZA

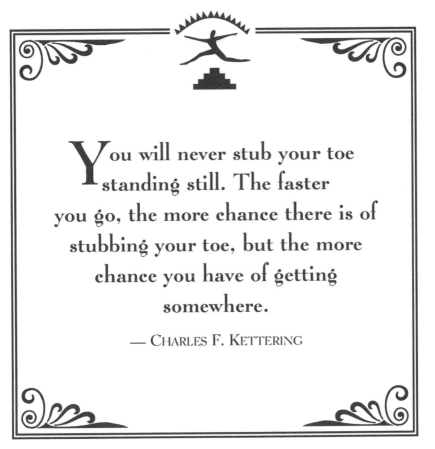

You will never stub your toe
standing still. The faster
you go, the more chance there is of
stubbing your toe, but the more
chance you have of getting
somewhere.

— CHARLES F. KETTERING

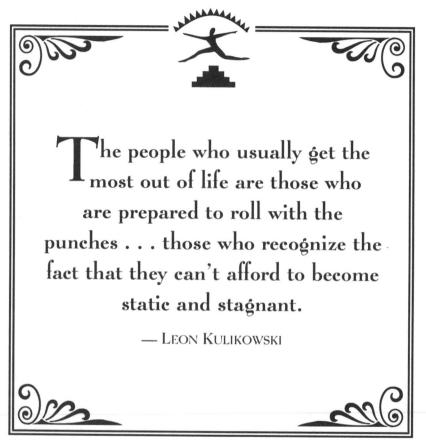

The people who usually get the most out of life are those who are prepared to roll with the punches . . . those who recognize the fact that they can't afford to become static and stagnant.

— LEON KULIKOWSKI

T rue success is obeying God.

— JOHN MAXWELL

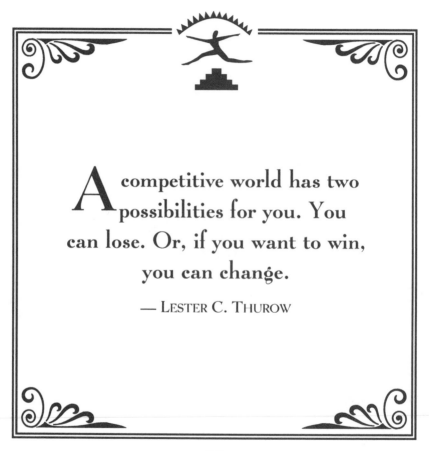

A competitive world has two possibilities for you. You can lose. Or, if you want to win, you can change.

— LESTER C. THUROW

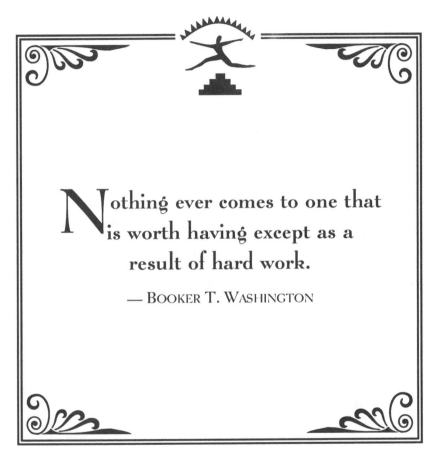

Nothing ever comes to one that is worth having except as a result of hard work.

— BOOKER T. WASHINGTON

Change is inevitable. Growth is optional.

— JOHN MAXWELL

The winner's edge is not in a gifted birth, a high IQ, or in talent. The winner's edge is all in the attitude, not aptitude. Attititude is the criterion for success. But you can't buy an attitude for a million dollars. Attitudes are not for sale.

— DENIS WAITLEY

Those who trust the LORD will find new strength.
They will be strong like eagles soaring upward on wings;
they will walk and run without getting tired.

— ISAIAH

Isaiah 40:31

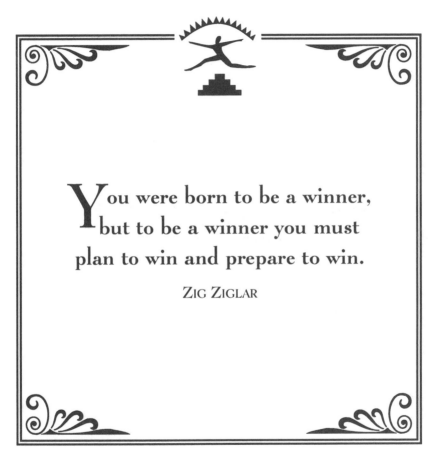

You were born to be a winner,
but to be a winner you must
plan to win and prepare to win.

ZIG ZIGLAR

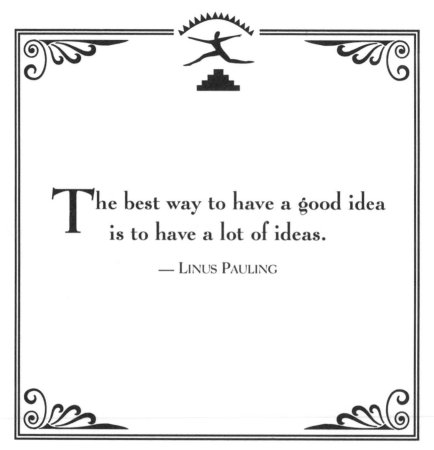

The best way to have a good idea
is to have a lot of ideas.

— LINUS PAULING

Complacency is the last hurdle
any winner, any team,
must overcome before attaining
potential greatness.

— PAT RILEY

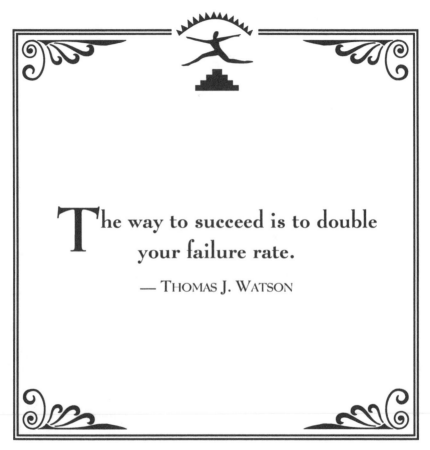

The way to succeed is to double your failure rate.

— THOMAS J. WATSON

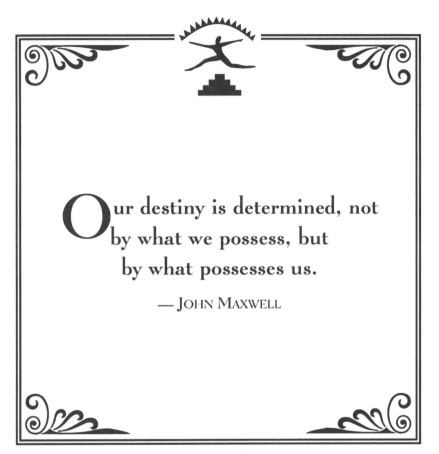

Our destiny is determined, not
by what we possess, but
by what possesses us.

— JOHN MAXWELL

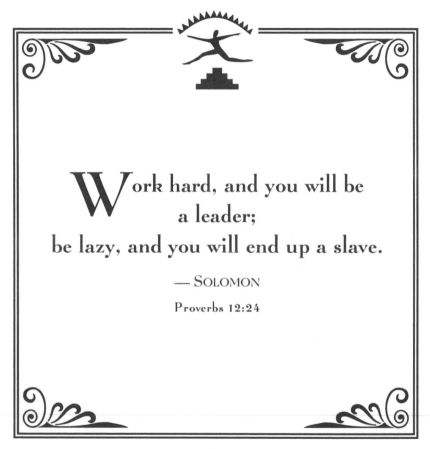

Work hard, and you will be
a leader;
be lazy, and you will end up a slave.

— SOLOMON

Proverbs 12:24

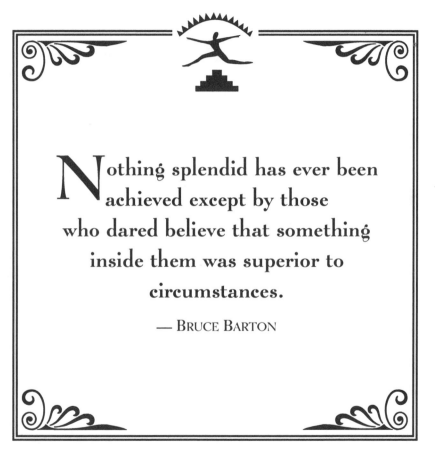

Nothing splendid has ever been achieved except by those who dared believe that something inside them was superior to circumstances.

— BRUCE BARTON

We exist temporarily through what we take, but we live forever through what we give.

— Douglas M. Lawson

Ease brings very little out
of people.

— JOHN MAXWELL

The greatest mistake one can make in life is to be continually fearing you will make one.

— ELBERT HUBBARD

I f God is your partner, make your plans big.

— D. L. MOODY

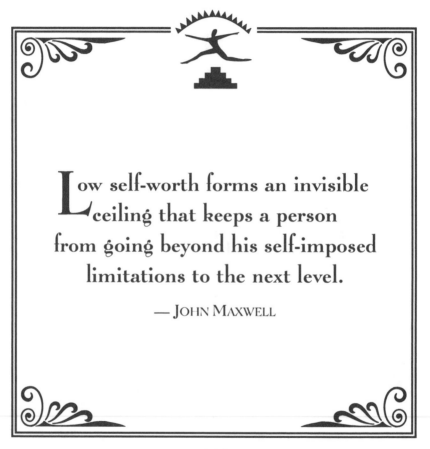

Low self-worth forms an invisible ceiling that keeps a person from going beyond his self-imposed limitations to the next level.

— JOHN MAXWELL

About the Author

Dr. John C. Maxwell is one of the top thinkers and equippers in the United States today in the area of personal and corporate leadership development. A dynamic motivational communicator, he speaks to over 150,000 people each year and is in great demand nationally and internationally on topics such as leadership, personal growth, attitude, relationship building, and Christian living.

He has spoken to such diverse organizations as Chick-fil-a, Amway, the Salvation Army, Creative Marketing, the Christian Booksellers Association, the National Collegiate Athletic Association, the Salem Communications Corporation, Home Interiors, and several professional sports teams. And he has frequently teamed with other notable business experts such as Zig Ziglar, Ken Blanchard, and Bob Buford.

John has over twenty-five years of experience in organizational leadership and holds an earned doctorate as well as two honorary ones. He is the author of over a dozen books with well over half a million in print. His titles include *Developing the Leader within You*, *Developing the Leaders around You*, *Breakthrough Parenting*, and *The Winning Attitude*.

ADDITIONAL LEADERSHIP, PERSONAL GROWTH, AND CHURCH GROWTH RESOURCES DEVELOPED BY JOHN C. MAXWELL ARE AVAILABLE FROM

INJOY

1-800-333-6506

INJOY is a San Diego-based Christian leadership organization dedicated to helping leaders reach their potential in ministry, business, and the family.

Through INJOY, John Maxwell offers a wide range of training seminars, books, videos, and audio cassette programs designed to increase an individual's ability to influence and lead others.

A unique resource is the INJOY Life Club, a one-hour equipping tape for pastors and Christian leaders taught by John Maxwell. It is currently mailed each month to over 10,000 subscribers, and that number is growing rapidly.

Another exciting resource offered by John Maxwell each month is "Maximum Impact," a leadership equipping tape for the business person working in the marketplace. It's like having a professional business seminar come to you every month!

To receive a catalog of resources available from INJOY or additional information regarding John Maxwell's speaking itinerary or motivational materials, please contact INJOY at:

INJOY

P.O. Box 19900
San Diego, CA 92159

800-333-6506
http://www.injoy.com

Let John Maxwell
take you to the next level!

John Maxwell has spent more than a quarter of a century helping people reach their potential. And he wants to do the same for you.

To become all you can be, read these insightful and motivating books by John Maxwell:

The Winning Attitude

Most people are very close to becoming the person God wants them to be. What enables them to take the next step? The right attitude! Let John show you how to be a winner.

Developing the Leader within You

Being a leader means more than having a position or title. True leadership is influence. Learn to lead from one of the nation's top experts. This book is a must for anyone in management, business, or any leadership position.

Developing the Leaders around You

Great leaders are never content to lead followers. They develop and lead other leaders. Receive inspired instruction on mentoring and team building from this gifted motivator.

**All three books are also available
on audio cassette.**
Published by Thomas Nelson Publishers.
Available in bookstores.